SURRENDER

FROM THE DEPTHS OF A HUNGRY WOMAN

EROTIC POETRY

Emily-Rose

From The Depths of A Hungry Woman
Copyright © 2025 by Emily-Rose Obscura

ISBN: 979-8-218-82148-7

TABLE OF CONTENTS

INTRODUCTION

I cannot sleep and when I do, even in my dreams I am being consumed. Consumed by the desire to have someone deep inside my being, penetrating my walls and bearing witness to what lingers in the deepest parts of me. There are no accidents in Divine orchestration.

I **surrender** to the hunger for something more.

FROM THE DEPTHS OF A HUNGRY WOMAN

I smile endearingly as your words arouse my ears

The sound of you is intoxicating

Won't you come whisper in my ear?

Come close,

I won't warn you that I bite

I see it clear, your eyes give it away

Screaming for me to have a taste

So, I will tear into you with the teeth the world tells me to hide

And you will surrender to every bite

DIVINE COUNTERPART

Only the depths of you could satiate a woman like me

Only a man like you could reach me so deep

Show me where my hunger leads

Are you hungry like me?

Let the world shun us and lock us away like the ravenous beast we'll become

When we finally come together as one

VICES

If they were to ask, I'd say I have no vices

But in the dead of night my secret comes to life

Erotic desire is my vice

For a man I do not know

But The Divine spoke of you as a foretold truth

I release my pleasure only to the thought of you

Class Act

Penetrate my walls with the girth of your virility

Thrust in me and feel the deepest parts of me

The only place you'll ever need is inside me

So come in me and make me your home

Thrust in me until I become undone

PLEASURE PEAK

Come with me,

I can take you for a ride

Hold me tight, Hold me still

I know it's close, I feel it too

Keep your eyes on me as we come undone

At the peak of pleasure,

We become one

TOUCH

With a delicate touch just as a spider spins a web,

I stroke the shaft of your desire as the tautness fills my hand

I guide your pleasure to a sweet release and let the proof wash over me

The salt and sweet like an ocean hitting the shore

Just a taste will leave me wanting more

Desire

Wind me up and I'll dance for you,

If that's what you desire

Tie me up and keep me bound,

If that's what you desire

Collar me as I crawl for you,

If that's what you desire

If you ask me what I want I will say my will is
your desire

COMING DOWN

Coming down for a taste

I want my mouth full of you

Every inch of your desire,

Saturated with the proof of my hunger

Filling my throat, making me whole

I'll take you as deep as you'll go

Watch me as I swallow you whole

DARKEST DREAMS

Guide me into your darkest dreams,

Make me your fantasy

Give me more than a gentle kiss,

Journey deep where no one's been

Hold me tight,

Hold me still

Make me take all of you

Come inside

Deep

Within

In your darkest dreams is where I long to be

MASOCHIST

Bring her out of me and let her play

The parasite that lives inside me,

Feed her pain

A fine line between pain and pleasure,

I feel them just the same

Show her no mercy,

She has no shame

Give her a taste of the pain she desperately craves

Be my escape and she'll leave me be

Until it's time again for her to feed

DANGEROUS THING

An anomaly in my design

Erotic desire plagues my mind

I ache for passion and an all-consuming love

I ache to devour and consume every part of you,

Until all that's left is a coalescence of us two

Know I will not feed on ordinary men

I only have a taste for you

MOUTHPIECE

Drink in The Divine from my dripping lips

Let my essence wash away your pain

Sink deep inside this righteous desire,

Feel yourself become renewed

Drown in the essence of something more

Everything you've been longing for is now yours

AURALISM

Whisper in my ear all the thoughts that are running through your mind

Tell me all the ways you want me

Talk me through the descent into your desire

I want to live among your fantasies

PRIMAL GAME

You growl against my aching skin,

I don't care for being locked in this cage within

So rip me apart from the inside out,

Make me new again

Claw at my skin

Take bites out of me,

I am yours to devour

I'll be your prey,

Pin me down and have a taste

My love is a primal game

AFTERTASTE

Tangled limbs,

We lay undone

I taste your dripping sweat on my tongue

The aftertaste of the Divine love we make

The taste of us becoming one

DEEP IN ME

Do you want to see what lies beneath my surface?

An array of things I hide,

Stored deep inside

Far from the light but you're a shadow that can reach the darkest parts of me

Come deep in me

Reveal all of me

Come find the dark world that hides beneath the surface of my light

ACHE

I yearn for your breath against my skin,

The weight of your body on mine

I ache,

I ache,

I ache for your embrace,

Proof that my maddening yearning was rooted in truth

I ache for all of you

THE DIVINE'S PROMISE

The Divine whispered of you as a promise,

A being that mirrors the madness I keep,

A being as devoted as me

I am here to claim what the Gods promised was mine

So come to me even if only in a dream.

THE DIVINE

PHANTOM

LOVER

EROTIC POETRY

Emily-Rose

INTRODUCTION

The earth beneath her feet pulsed, as if the soil itself desired to be close to her. The garden around her was not just alive, it was worshiping her.

The air wrapped around her like invisible hands desperate to feel every inch of her and she surrendered to every touch. *So long she had been running, but what was it she had been running from?*

Her thoughts popped like delicate bubbles in the intoxicating air.

This is not a place for thoughts.

A soft breeze swept across her, teasing her until she moaned. *Was she ever running from something, or was she running to get here?*

This is not a place for thoughts.

Ecstasy overcame her as the garden's caresses became hungry. She glanced between her parted thighs, a dim, golden light flickered in the distance. *Has that light always been there?*

This is not a place for thoughts.

She moaned as the weight of the garden's essence pressed against her until it was impossible to ignore. Every door inside her opened wide, aching and begging to be explored. She melted into the garden until she no longer knew if she was being embraced or consumed.

———————

In the distance, a candle flickered in a tall window.

He watched her through the glass, his face hidden behind the golden candlelight. The garden he had prepared for her was finally alive.

She was home.

Are you even real?

DIVINE EROTICA

Erotica has been expressed in many ways throughout the history of literature, and I wanted to bring my own version of it into the world. I believe sexuality is sacred, an expression of the soul's yearning to merge, to create, and to remember its divine essence through touch and devotion. In my world erotica does not exist without divinity and love. Through my writing I aim to show the passion and fullness that can exist when love, flesh, and spirit intertwine as one.

ABOUT AUTHOR

Emily-Rose is an introvert, a daydreamer, and a writer whose words often come to her in dreams. She has devoted her life to self-discovery; walking a path shaped by spirituality and solitude. Each story she writes is a step on her own journey shaped by vulnerability and the deep desire to learn who she truly is. Outside of writing, Emily-Rose is a passionate adventurer drawn to movement and art. Whether it's hiking remote trails, painting in her studio, or getting lost in her words, she's constantly chasing moments that ignite her creativity. Through her writing, Emily-Rose invites you to journey with her into erotic passion, self-discovery, and the truth that lingers in longing.